Ruth and Esther
Bible Study
BSBP Series
(Bible Studies for Busy People)

BSBP SERIES - BIBLE STUDY
Ruth and Esther
CONTENTS

BSBP SERIES

(BIBLE STUDIES FOR BUSY PEOPLE)

The world is becoming increasingly busy and as Christians we are not immune from this. There always seems to be so much to do but so little time to do it! However, many of us love the Bible and would like to have more time to study it. So............

The BSBP series has been prepared just for people like us – those who have a real desire to study the Bible but find they simply do not have enough time.

Do you want to study the Bible? Have you been put off by the length - and depth - of many of the books that are on offer? If your answer is 'yes' to these questions then the BSBP series is for you!

You will be taken step by step through your chosen book of the Bible - just 10 studies with 10 questions in each study. The brief supporting notes, will keep you focused on the job in hand. You will quickly and easily get a sound grasp of the subject matter - without having to use hours and hours of your valuable time!

There are several studies available and full details can be found on Amazon.co.uk or Amazon.com. You can also find full details on www.howdoiknowbooks.com. All the studies are ideal for both personal development and for stimulating thoughtful discussion within small groups.

The books of Ruth and Esther are very interesting, encouraging and challenging. I hope you will enjoy using this study as much as I have enjoyed writing it!

May God bless you as you study His Word and by so doing increase in your knowledge of Him.

Margaret Weston

INTRODUCTION TO RUTH AND ESTHER

What a wonderful example we have in Ruth and Esther of so many beautiful qualities of one who is committed to the will of God in his or her life. Qualities which are equally important for both men and women who love God and know Jesus as their Saviour but who also want Him to be Lord of their lives.

We see faithfulness, wisdom, humility, courage and many other traits demonstrated by these women who, in God's ways, found themselves in extraordinary circumstances. Then, through their commitment and faithfulness in those circumstances, they also found themselves as a very significant part of God's purpose and plans with their names recorded in history. They are the only women to have a whole book of the Bible devoted to them. What great women they were but I doubt if they realised what a tremendous impact they would have on future generations. Ruth is found in Matthew 1 in the genealogy, the 'royal line' which led to the birth of Christ, and Esther saved the nation of the Jews from destruction.

Ruth's husband had died leaving her alone and destitute. At that time and in that culture, to be a widow meant being destitute – without anyone to provide security in the form of food and shelter and no-one to give protection from physical harm. Ruth had every reason to follow Orpah, who went back to her own country in the hope of finding another husband from her own people. But, her commitment to Naomi would not allow her to do this 'where you go I will go and where you stay I will stay. Your people will be my people and your God my God. Where you die I will die and there will I be buried'. Her prospects at that time with Naomi were for a life alone without a husband, and probably also in poverty. Yet, she did not take the easy way out and go with Orpah, she refused to leave Naomi. She had made a commitment to Naomi and she was trusting in Naomi's God and her commitment was absolute. Are we tempted sometimes to take the easy way out and in so doing forfeit the fullest blessing of God in our lives? Or, are we prepared to commit ourselves to the will of God irrespective of the possible consequences. So often God's way is the harder way but it is also the way to the fullest blessing. If we want to follow Jesus, then we must be prepared for the refining process which so often is needed to shape our character and strengthen our faith.

Esther's experience and background were quite different from Ruth but she also came to a point in her life where she had a very difficult decision to make. At that time and in that culture in Persia, no-one was allowed to approach the king without his invitation – not even the queen. If anyone did so they could be put to death. The king had already shown how ruthless he could be when he banished Queen Vashti from the kingdom because she disobeyed him. Now Esther had to decide if she was willing to approach him in order to save her people from destruction and death. It must have gone through her mind how much there was to lose. In many ways she had everything. She had beauty, wealth, power and the king had been very pleased with her. Why should she risk everything? But, that was exactly what she was prepared to do because of her commitment and, no doubt her love, for her people – the Jews. She says 'I will go to the king, even though it is against the law – and if I perish, I perish.' What an example for us when we are faced with a tricky decision. Will we run away from the problem, or will we stand up for what we believe and be prepared for the consequences whatever they may be.

Ruth and Esther are there to challenge us to be Christians who are committed to Jesus Christ and be prepared to do His will whatever the cost. They were both prepared to choose the more difficult path regardless of the consequences because of their faith in God. What about you?

This Bible study consists of 10 studies, 4 of which focus on the book of Ruth and 6 on the book of Esther. Whilst we look at each book separately, it is also important to focus on the differences and the similarities between these two women, both of whom were so important in the purpose and plans of God. As we study these women we can learn so much from them.

However, at the same time it is a sobering thought that we do have a choice. We can always choose to follow God's way or our own way – we can be part of His glorious plan or we can turn aside. In either case, God is not thwarted and if we turn away He is able to use someone else. As Mordecai said to Esther, ' For if you remain silent at this time, relief and deliverance for the Jews will arise from another place, but you and your father's family will perish. And who knows, but that you have come to royal position for such a time as this.'

So, let's use these studies to encourage ourselves and one another to seek God's will in our lives and to remain in it. To be prepared to stand firm whatever the cost may seem to be, because by faith we know that He loves us and will only do what is best for us. 'If God be for us, who can be against us? He who did not spare His own Son, but gave Him up for us all – how will He not also, along with Him, graciously give us all things?' Romans 8:31-32.

Study 1 – Ruth Chapter 1
Commitment

Read Ruth chapter 1

Discuss/think about

Identify the different people in this chapter and discuss/think about some of their characteristics. How and why does Ruth stand out from the others?

1. When we experience trouble in our lives we can react in different ways. What are these different ways and what are the possible consequences of each reaction?

2. Why might we choose to run from our problems as Naomi and Elimilech did?

3. Was there anything wrong about Naomi's decision to go back to Bethlehem?

4. How did Naomi react to her problems?

5. What happens when we start to concentrate more on ourselves and our problems than we do on God and His purpose and glory?

6. By going to Bethlehem what would Ruth leave behind?

7. What does Ruth's decision and her words reveal about her character?

8. Have you ever made sacrifices, or seen someone close to you make them, in order to honour a commitment you/they have made?

9. In what areas of our lives is it important to be faithful? Why?

10. How is Jesus a perfect example for us of commitment, loyalty and faithfulness?

Don't forget to pray

The Christian life is sometimes said to be a series of new beginnings. With God it is never too late to start over again, to make a fresh commitment, to confess our past mistakes and begin again. Think about where you are in your life at this present time and ask the Holy Spirit to guide you in the will of God, to help you make right commitments and then to be true to them whatever the cost.

Notes for Ruth - Chapter 1
Commitment

In this chapter we meet several characters and we can learn something from each of them. First, Elimilech who left Bethlehem and his own people because he thought he could do better elsewhere. Then his wife Naomi who went with him but was later left without either her husband or her two sons and became very bitter about what she considered the Lord had done to her.

Next, the two sons who, as a result of their father's decision to go to Moab, ended up marrying Moabite women. (Jews were forbidden to marry Moabite women, see Deuteronomy 7:3). Then we meet Orpah, who went some of the way with Naomi towards Bethlehem but was essentially a weak woman who was persuaded to take the easier path and return to her own people. Finally, Ruth showing faithfulness, love, commitment and other wonderful qualities as an example of a true woman of God.

Bethlehem means 'house of bread' and yet there was a famine! Sometimes God had to discipline Israel because of their disobedience but He remains faithful throughout and we see in verse 6 that Naomi heard that God had provided food for His people. During the famine Elimilech and Naomi had decided to leave Bethlehem and go to Moab. They had tried to run away from their problems only to find that in Moab things were much worse. Elimilech died, the two sons married Moabite women and then the two sons also died.

So, Naomi was bitter about how things had turned out but in many ways they had been as a result of the decision to leave Bethlehem in the first place. How often we blame God for things when they are really a result of our own actions! However, He is the only One who can bring victory out of failure and we should always remember that, 'all things work for the good of those who love God' Romans 8:28. All things means exactly that – *all* things!

We need to ask why Naomi decided to return to Bethlehem. Was it only for the food which was available or did she have any sense of her failure in turning away from God's way? Why did she encourage her two daughters-in-law to leave her? If returning to Bethlehem was right for Naomi, why was it not also right for Ruth and Orpah? What an opportunity Naomi had to return to the Lord and take with her two trophies of grace for God's glory! Perhaps Naomi was ashamed that her sons had married women from Moab and if they returned with her to Bethlehem the failure of her family would be exposed. In any case, Orpah decided to take the more comfortable option while Ruth stood firm in her decision to stick with Naomi.

It seems that Ruth now had her own knowledge of Naomi's God – 'your God will be my God'. Ruth was not a Jew but God in His grace 'grafted' her in (Romans 11:17) to the royal line, 'the genealogy of Jesus Christ' (Matthew 1). What a wonderful example of someone who is a loyal and faithful friend and whose commitment to Naomi and Naomi's God affected the generations to come, right through to the birth of Jesus Christ.

Study 2 – Ruth Chapter 2
Humility

Read Ruth chapter 2

Discuss/think about

What character traits are displayed in this chapter by each of the following people:- a) Ruth; b) Naomi and c) Boaz.

1. Read Leviticus 19:9-10. Do these verses help to explain some of Ruth's actions in this chapter?

2. What kind of work might be similar to 'gleaning' today?

3. Many Bible students believe that Boaz is a 'type' or 'picture' of the Lord Jesus Christ in this book. Why do you think this is? (Consider the relationship of Jesus Christ to His Church and to us as individuals.)

4. How do you think Ruth demonstrated her faith in the God of Israel? Look at James chapter 2 verse 20. Do you see any connection?

5. Where and how do we see God at work through various circumstances in this chapter?

6. Discuss examples of how God has worked in your life through various circumstances.

7. Are there 'accidents' or 'coincidences' in the life of a true Christian?

8. What change(s) do you see in Naomi in this chapter? Why do you think this is?

9. Think of some examples in our lives today where a character like 'Ruth' could help a 'Naomi'.

10. What characteristic displayed by Ruth in this chapter would you most like to have?

Don't forget to pray

'For those God foreknew He also predestined to be conformed to the likeness of His Son'. Romans 8:29. God's purpose is to make us more like Jesus and He uses our circumstances to help to achieve this. Ask the Holy Spirit to work in you and through you to make you more like Jesus.

Notes for Ruth - Chapter 2
Humility

Ruth continues to show many beautiful traits and we see obedience, humility and patience especially in this chapter. We see Naomi moving from bitterness to words of blessing (verse 20) as a result of Ruth's actions and we are introduced to Boaz, a man of great kindness and grace.

Leviticus 19:9-10 and Deuteronomy 25:5-10 help us to understand some of the Jewish customs which come into this chapter and the book of Ruth. The first reference is about the practice of leaving 'gleanings' for the poor when harvesting the fields and the second reference explains what should happen to a widow. We see God at work through these customs and in the circumstances that form part of Ruth's life. She would have had no idea that through all these circumstances she was to become part of the 'royal line' which would eventually lead to the birth of Christ!

It is interesting to see how Ruth's relationship with Boaz develops throughout this book. In chapter one Ruth did not even know that Boaz existed. Now in chapter two she meets him but is just a poor labourer in one of his fields. Watch with interest how this relationship develops in the next two chapters and think of this as a picture of your relationship with Jesus! Keep in mind too throughout the book the lovely picture shown of the relationship of our Lord Jesus Christ with His Bride, His Church. Boaz is the 'kinsman-redeemer' in this chapter and this is developed further in the next two chapters. Christ has been 'made in human likeness' (Philippians 2:7), our 'kinsman' and He has redeemed us! Romans 8:29 tells us, 'For those God foreknew he also predestined to be conformed to the likeness of his Son, that he might be the firstborn among many brothers'.

See how Boaz takes the initiative in this chapter, he speaks with Ruth, he makes sure she has food and drink, he encourages her and he makes sure she will be safe and well-cared for in his fields. All Ruth has to do is to continue to be obedient, work faithfully and trust in the 'God of Israel under whose wings you have come to take refuge' – verse 12.

How wonderful to have such faith in God that we can trust Him in all our circumstances *whatever they may be,* knowing that He has a perfect plan and purpose for our lives, the end result of which will be that we are formed 'in the likeness of His Son'. We can learn from Ruth to trust that God is at work in all our circumstances and so can trust Him totally with every aspect of our lives. Ruth did not look back at her tragic past or focus on herself and her present problems. She focused on Boaz and his kindness. In Hebrews 12:2 we are told to 'fix our eyes on Jesus' and as we do this and believe on His word and in His promises we shall be blessed beyond our expectations.

Study 3 – Ruth Chapter 3
Obedience

Read Ruth chapter 3

Discuss/think about

Ruth says to Naomi 'I will do whatever you say'. Was Ruth taking a risk in this chapter by obeying Naomi? Why do you think she was prepared to do this?

1. Ruth was told to wash herself before going into the presence of Boaz. How is this a picture of what we should do as we meet with Jesus? Look at 2 Corinthians 7:1.

2. Ruth also 'perfumed' or 'anointed' herself in her preparation to meet Boaz. What does this represent for us? See 1 John 2:20.

3. What would the change of clothing mean for Ruth and what does it mean for us today? Read Isaiah 64:6 and 2 Corinthians 5:21.

4. Read Leviticus 25:47-50 which helps us to understand the law of the kinsman-redeemer. How does Boaz react when he finds Ruth at his feet?

5. How does Ruth behave throughout the encounter and what does this tell us about her character?

6. What do you think 'spreading a garment' (v9) over someone would represent at that time? What might it represent today? Ezekiel 16:8 may help.

7. Boaz says 'don't be afraid'. Does this remind you of other scriptures where we are told not to be afraid? Do you find this easy? Why/Why not?

8. How does Naomi react when Ruth returns?

9. How do you react if you are told to 'wait'?

10. Read Psalm 37:5. Can you see a link with this chapter of Ruth? Can you see a link to your own life?

Don't forget to pray

Ask yourself whether you are prepared to put yourself at the feet of Jesus and submit to His way. Are you able to 'wait patiently' (Psalm 37:7) for Him to act in your life? Meditate on Psalm 37 verses 1-11 and think about the way Ruth has behaved in this book so far. Ask the Holy Spirit to make any changes necessary in you – but make sure you are prepared for the answers!

Notes on Ruth - Chapter 3
Obedience

We continue to see the progress in the relationship between Ruth and Boaz as we move into chapter 3 i.e. in chapter 1 she does not even know that Boaz exists, then in chapter 2 she is a poor labourer who is shown kindness by Boaz. Now in chapter 3 we see Ruth prepared to submit herself to Boaz and put herself at his feet.

In those days it would have been the parents who arranged marriages and so Naomi would not have been out of place with her suggestions. Naomi would also have known the laws and customs which were appropriate in this situation. For Ruth though, as a 'new' believer, some of these things may have seemed quite strange. In her eyes she may have been taking a huge risk. What if Boaz rejected her? She may have thought that surely there could have been another way forward. However, because of her faith in Naomi's God ('your God will be my God') she was prepared to take this risk.

The chapter begins with Ruth making preparation before she goes into the presence of Boaz. We cannot simply rush into the presence of God trusting in our own righteousness or our own ideas. We have to be obedient to Him. So, we have to be *washed* from our sins, *anointed* by the Holy Spirit (oil often represents the Holy Spirit in Scripture) and we have to put on Christ's righteousness rather than be clothed in the 'filthy rags' of our own righteousness. See Isaiah 64:6 and Revelation 19:8.

The law of the kinsman-redeemer is explained in other Old Testament scriptures – see Leviticus 25:47-60 - and to spread a cloak over someone would mean claiming that person for oneself. Ruth had come under the wings of the God of Israel for protection (see chapter 2:12) and now Boaz was agreeing to spread his garment over her.

We see a wonderful example in this chapter of obedience, submission and patience. A beautiful picture of how our lives can bring glory to God if we are willing to submit to Him so that His will can be done. God is able to use our circumstances to lead us, to guide us and to change us to become more like Jesus. Ruth had to have patience while everything was worked out and so do we! What a different end to this story we may have seen if Ruth had insisted on her own will and followed her own ideas. If she had been unwilling to do the work of a poor labourer, or unwilling to listen to Naomi, or unwilling to put herself at the feet of Boaz, then we are unlikely to have seen the lovely end to this book. Ruth has baby Obed who became the grandfather of King David!

God is able to abundantly bless those who seek to live obedient lives and those around them are often blessed because of this. Naomi was changed because of Ruth and we see Naomi's interest, enthusiasm and excitement coming through in verses 16-18. What a contrast to the early part of chapter 2 where it is Ruth who takes the initiative and Naomi merely says 'go ahead'. We all have an influence on those around us in some way, whether it be for good or bad.

Finally we see at the end of the chapter how Ruth has to wait for Boaz to act. How difficult it is sometimes for us to put matters into God's hands and simply wait for Him to act! Boaz kept his word – how much more then will God keep His promises and work out everything for our good – Romans 8:28.

Study 4 – Ruth Chapter 4
Joy

Read Ruth chapter 4

Discuss/think about

Think about Ruth in chapter 1 of this book and compare and contrast that with how she is in this chapter. Discuss what relevance this may have with our own lives.

1. What do you think is the meaning of 'redemption'?

2. Why do you think that the 'kinsman-redeemer' in this chapter is likened to Jesus Christ?

3. Have you been redeemed and if so, what does this mean to you personally?

4. Read Deuteronomy 25:5-10 and Leviticus 25:23-34. How do these scriptures help to explain some of what is happening in this chapter?

5. What characteristics of God (e.g. His grace) have come through in this book in His dealings with Ruth?

6. How did God use the birth of baby Obed as a source of blessing, both at the time of his birth and then for future generations?

7. Can you see any similarities between Ruth who was the bride of Boaz, and the Church as the bride of Christ?

8. What similarities have you seen in this book of Ruth, between Boaz and his relationship with Ruth, and Jesus and His relationship with you?

9. As a result of Ruth's commitment and obedience she left behind a wonderful legacy for others. What legacy would you like to leave behind?

10. What have you learned from studying this book of Ruth? Will it help you to deepen your relationship with Jesus?

Don't forget to pray

Ruth's commitment to God and her willingness to submit to His will in her life made a tremendous difference to her own life, the lives of those around her and the lives of future generations. Make some time to come before God and reflect on this. Are you willing to make a full commitment to God so that He can use you to bless others in a wonderful way?

Notes for Ruth - Chapter 4
Joy

What a wonderful result and what joy we have in this chapter following Ruth's commitment and obedience to the will of God in her life. Chapter 1 starts with three funerals but in this chapter we have a wedding and the birth of a baby. God abundantly blesses those who seek to live obedient lives.

The word 'redeem' means 'to set free by paying a price'. We find words like redeem, buy and purchase several times in this chapter. There can be no redemption unless a price is paid. 'The ransom (or redemption) for a life is costly' (Psalm 49:8) and 'without the shedding of blood there is no forgiveness' (Hebrews 9:22) are two scriptures among many which illustrate the tremendous cost to God of redeeming us. God is a God of love but also of justice and righteousness. God was therefore obeying His own laws when He accomplished our salvation in Christ.

It is interesting to note that the kinsman-redeemer had to be a near-relative, had to pay the price for redemption and had to be willing to do so. Anselm of Canterbury said, when explaining why God became man and died for us, that 'none but God *can* make satisfaction (for the debt owed) and none but man *ought* to make satisfaction, therefore it is necessary for the God-man to make it'.* It has to be a perfect spotless *man*, our kinsman, who paid the price for our sins in order to satisfy a holy, righteous and perfect God.

The laws concerning the kinsman-redeemer and marriage of a widow are found in Leviticus 25:23-34 and Deuteronomy 25:5-10. The purpose of such laws was to preserve the name and protect the property of families in Israel. Naomi and Boaz would have been well aware of these laws and were following the correct procedures. There is a reason for both the laws in the Old Testament and the moral 'laws' or behaviours which should govern our lives today. They are all for our blessing and the blessing of those around us.

We see God at work in Ruth's life in love, grace, mercy and power. His grace and love to one who was outside the chosen Jewish race but brought in through mercy and power to form part of the royal line leading to the birth of Christ. Baby Obed became the grandfather of King David and we see the genealogy outlined at the end of this book and then in its completeness in Matthew chapter 1.

There are many references in Scripture to the bride and the bridegroom and images of the Church as the bride of Christ – e.g. Ephesians 5:23-27; Revelation 19:6-9 and Rev 21:2. Christ died for the Church, Ephesians 5:25, He cleanses it through His word (v26) and He will one day present it to Himself in glory 'without stain or blemish' (v27). Many Bible scholars have seen this picture illustrated in Ruth.

So, we should never under-estimate the love, the mercy, the power and the grace of God as He works in our lives to fulfil His glorious purposes. Our part is to submit to Him and allow Him to have full sway in our lives. Ruth was prepared to commit herself completely to God's will in her life and she was abundantly blessed as a result as well as becoming a blessing herself to those around her and generations to come. In a similar way, God can use us today if we are prepared to submit to Him.

* Anselm of Canterbury – The Major Works p320 (Oxford University Press)

Study 5 – Esther Chapters 1 & 2
Preparation

Read Esther chapters 1 & 2

Discuss/think about

Identify the different people you have just read about and discuss/think about which of these people you consider to have the main, or major, parts to play in these two chapters. How significant are the roles of the others who seem to have a smaller part to play?

1. Where can you see God at work in these chapters?

2. Identify which of the people mentioned are Jews. Does God only work through the Jewish people in these chapters?

3. Can God work today through people who are not Christians?

4. How did the king's anger and the banishment of Queen Vashti affect God's plans?

5. Are God's plans thwarted by ungodly leaders of nations today?

6. Why do you think Esther and Mordecai concealed their identity?

7. What do you think Esther thought and felt as she was being prepared for her meeting with the king? Do you think she knew she would one day be used by God in a very special and important way?

8. Why do you think there was no reward or special honour for Mordecai when he uncovered the plot against the king (2:22-23)?

9. What can we learn for ourselves today from the way in which God was acting in the lives of Mordecai and Esther?

10. How can faith in the providence and sovereignty of God affect us in our everyday lives today?

Don't forget to pray

God knows how to move you when the time comes for you to be moved and He knows what is happening to you and what should be happening for you. We have to trust God because there is nothing He doesn't know and He can change things in an instant – if it is His will. Do you have the faith to accept this? If not, ask God to give you such faith so that you can trust Him in, and for, everything.

Notes for Esther - Chapters 1 & 2
Preparation

Ruth and Esther were completely different people with completely different backgrounds. One was a Gentile, one was a Jewess; the background for Ruth was a Jewish village and a simple life. For Esther it was a bustling Gentile city and the politics and problems surrounding life in a palace with a sovereign monarch in control. However, the same God was present and working in both their lives and in the lives of those around them, so as to accomplish His plans and purposes. God is mentioned several times in the book of Ruth but it has often been noted that His name does not appear even once in the book of Esther. Whether we accept Him or not, whether we mention His name or not, God is always there with His eye on each of us and 'He works out everything in conformity with the purpose of His will' (Ephesians 1:11). We cannot really read this book without being conscious of God. We can see Him behind the scenes even if He is not mentioned.

God was working and caring for His people Israel and fulfilling His promise to Abraham (Genesis 12:2-3). Not only is He working through the Jewish people in this book but He is also using others to accomplish His will, even if such people were unaware of it. Proverbs 21:1 says, 'The king's heart is in the hand of the Lord; He directs it like a watercourse wherever He pleases'. Thus we can see that the king's anger and the banishment of Vashti, to make way for Esther, were used by God even though the king was unaware of this and made his decisions of his own freewill. The sovereignty of God is a wonderful comfort in troubled times in the world because His people can trust Him to accomplish His purposes irrespective, or indeed even by using, those in positions of leadership who do not know God.

Esther and Mordecai were not perfect but they were prepared to be used by God in order to save the Jewish people from destruction. God will use us if we are prepared to commit ourselves to Him and His purposes. Esther may have had no idea that she was being placed in the king's harem in order to fulfil a special mission from God. Maybe she wondered what use she was there, but God had it all in hand and was preparing her for a very special purpose. Ruth had to go through a period of preparation before meeting Boaz and Esther had to go through a period of preparation before being able to act for God. In most cases, we also have to go through a period of preparation before we can be used by God. Even if we have a special gift, we still need preparation before we rush off to use it! Esther had to be patient during this period of preparation and perhaps we do too! God is preparing each of us, if we are committed to His will, and will use us if, or when, the time comes.

Mordecai could have been most downcast when he uncovered the plot against the king and received no thanks or recognition for this. He could have given up and thought 'what's the point' but he continued doing his job in the right way and there is no indication that he was aggrieved by this non-recognition. Are we prepared to go on working for God irrespective of whether we are noticed or recognised for what we do? Are we prepared to have faith in God that He will use what we do for Him for His glory and to achieve His purposes even if no-one else seems to notice?

We should be encouraged by these chapters and this book of Esther which shows us how a sovereign God is always in control, irrespective of how it might look to us. He WILL work out everything for our eternal good (Romans 8:28) and He WILL 'work out everything in conformity with the purpose of His will' (Ephesians 1:11).

Study 6 – Esther Chapters 3 & 4
Courage

Read Esther chapters 3 & 4

Discuss/think about

Why was Haman so against Mordecai and the Jews? Discuss/think about Haman's plot against the Jews and consider what would have happened if he had been able to exterminate the Jewish nation.

1. Haman was promoted and Mordecai was not even thanked for revealing the plot against the king (previous chapter). Can you see any similarities with this situation in life today?

2. When and why did Mordecai reveal that he was a Jew?

3. We are taught in the New Testament that Christians should normally submit to those in authority. When might this not be the case? Mordecai would not bow to Haman. Can you think of any other similar examples in history or in the Bible?

4. Why did Mordecai act as he did at the king's gate?

5. Who was Hathach and what was his role? (Did you even notice his name when the chapter was being read?!)

6. Do you think Hathach realised what an important role he was playing in God's plan to defeat Haman and save the Jews? What significance do you see in this for our lives today?

7. Can you think of any other people who seem 'insignificant' either in the Bible or in history who have been used to accomplish God's plans and purposes?

8. Why did Esther ask the Jews to fast?

9. How did Esther demonstrate her absolute commitment to do God's will?

10. How might our commitment to God's will be demonstrated in our lives today?

Don't forget to pray

Can you think of a time when God prepared you for something that happened later on in your life? Do you think God may be preparing you now for something later? Whether the answer is yes or no to these questions, ask Him for patience and trust as He works in YOUR life to accomplish HIS plans.

Notes for Esther - Chapters 3 & 4
Courage

Haman was an 'Agagite' which may mean he came from a district known as 'Agag'. However, many Bible scholars see this description meaning that he was a descendant from Agag, who was the king of the Amalekites (1 Samuel 15:8). If this is the case, then we can more easily understand why there was such feeling between Haman and Mordecai. The Amalekites had been enemies of the Israelites for a long time, right back to the exodus from Egypt (see Deut 25:17-19). Saul was told to completely destroy the Amalekites – 1 Samuel 15:3 – but did not do so.

It is unthinkable that Haman's plot would be successful - the Jews were God's chosen people and if they had been destroyed then His plans would have been thwarted and He would not have kept His promise to Abraham. It is doubtful that anyone in this book would have had any idea of how things would work out and yet Mordecai and Esther were prepared to trust God and act in faith, irrespective of the outcome.

We might wonder how Mordecai felt when Haman was promoted and yet Mordecai was not even thanked for revealing the plot against the king. How often today we see good men and women seemingly overlooked and those who are wrong are promoted or put into positions of responsibility. Sometimes we have to wait a long time, and sometimes our good deeds are never recognised by men – but we can be sure that God knows and that should be our reward. Eventually Mordecai was recognised but a lot had to happen beforehand.

We need care when looking at Scripture so that we do not take one part in isolation. As Christians we should normally 'bow' to those in positions of authority and respect them in such a position. We should only not do so if we have clear guidance from God and know clearly, according to God's word, why we are taking such a stand. Mordecai came to the point where he simply had to reveal that he was a Jew and show publicly his sorrow at what was happening. Martin Luther is an example in history of one man refusing to bow down under 'authority' and retract what he had written. Sometimes we do well to remember the well known saying that 'all that is required for evil to triumph is for good men to do nothing'.

It is a great encouragement to see the part played by Hathach in this book of Esther. Seemingly insignificant and playing a minor part in relative obscurity, so much was hinged upon what he did. It is doubtful he realised how important his task was – he was simply doing his job. (The little girl in 2 Kings 5:2-3 who had a vital role in curing Naaman of his leprosy is another example.) How often we may carry out small tasks which we think are very insignificant – but it could well be that God is using us in a vital part of His great plans and purposes!

Esther realised the enormity of her task – if I perish, I perish – and she knew she could not do this on her own. She had to have others interceding with God on her behalf – showing their sincerity, commitment and care about what was happening by fasting. How often do we fast and pray today? How often are we so distressed at what is happening against God in our world that we feel we must fast and pray?

There is much we can learn from these chapters. God has a divine purpose which involves this world and He will accomplish it. He uses Christians and non-Christians in ways we do not fully understand. Our part however is to willingly be part of His plans and purposes. Not so much what should I do and where shall I live, but *for whom* do I live, work and act. Do I want to be part of God's plans and purposes? If I do and am prepared to commit myself to Him then He will surely use me.

Study 7 – Esther Chapter 5
Wisdom

Read Esther chapter 5

Discuss/think about

How do you think Esther felt as she stood waiting in front of the king's hall? How would you have felt? Think of a challenging situation you may have faced – how did you feel and how did you prepare for it?

1. What can we learn in this chapter about Esther's character?

2. Why do you think Esther did not immediately put her request to the king?

3. How can we see God working and over-seeing events in this chapter?

4. Read James 2:14-25 and discuss/think about how this passage could relate to this chapter of Esther.

5. How should we balance prayer and action in our Christian lives today?

6. How did God honour Esther's faith and courage?

7. What characteristics are displayed by Haman?

8. We learned from the book of Ruth that each of us has an influence on those around us – which may be good or bad. How can we see this demonstrated here by the different characters in this chapter?

9. Why is God so against pride (Proverbs 8:13)? How do you react when you see pride in others? How can family and friends help or hinder us in dealing with pride?

10. Look at James 1:5 and Proverbs 4:5.   How is wisdom demonstrated in this chapter and why should we ask God for it?

Don't forget to pray

Find some time to read and think about Proverbs chapters 1-4. Ask God to give you His wisdom as you seek His will for your life. Ask Him to show you how you can be part of His purposes and His plans.

Notes for Esther - Chapter 5
Wisdom

Scripture does not tell us how Esther felt as she waited but she must have been concerned about what would happen. She had already said 'if I perish, I perish' and was therefore prepared for this. She knew how unpredictable the king was and how he was prone to outbursts of anger. She would have known what had happened to Vashti and she was well aware of the law which said that anyone approaching the king without being summoned would be put to death. In spite of all this she was prepared to act, which showed her faith, her courage, her commitment to God and her love for her people the Jews, She also had the wisdom to act in the right way which had no doubt been given her by God.

Faith often requires us to act which is why James says that faith without works is dead. Esther was prepared to put her faith into action. Somebody had to act or disaster would occur. She had asked her people to fast and pray and now the time for action had come. Her faith was not 'blind faith' because she would have known of God's covenant with the Jews. She would also have known from history that the God of Israel was a forgiving God who heard His people when they humbled themselves before Him and prayed. Likewise, today we know the promises of God and we know that He hears prayer. Are we prepared to be like Esther and step out in faith in spite of the possible consequences?

We need wisdom from God to know when and how to act and this comes through prayer. Prayer is vital at all times and we always need to pray (1 Thessalonians 5:17). Action is not always appropriate and waiting can be just as hard at times. There is a well-known 'prayer' which says 'God grant me the serenity to accept the things I cannot change, the courage to change the things that I can, and the WISDOM to know the difference'.

If Esther had simply rushed in and put her request to the king in a public place and in front of others he may have reacted in a very different way. He may have considered what Esther was saying as gossip or enmity against his favoured servant Haman. Esther was acting with God's wisdom which allowed another night to pass during which God was working with the king. We will see that when the request was finally put to the king it was at a time when he had just honoured Mordecai for what he had done. So we can see God acting behind the scenes in all these events in order to bring about His plan and purpose for the Jews.

We see many bad characteristics displayed by Haman, (see Proverbs 6:16-19!) particularly malice, but most of all we see pride. Proverbs 11:2 tells us that 'when pride comes then comes disgrace' and we can see this demonstrated in what eventually happens to Haman. We also see how his bad influence affected his family and friends. Conversely we can see how Esther affected those around her for good.

We know from the Scriptures that God hates pride (e.g. it is the first on the list in Proverbs 6:16-19; see also Mark 9:34 and Luke 18:11-14). Pride caused the fall of man in the garden of Eden ('you will be like God') and it seems that it was pride that first caused the devil to sin (Isaiah 14:14 'I will be like the most High'). We need to be constantly watchful for pride in ourselves and pray that God will preserve us from it through the work of the Holy Spirit.

Study 8 – Esther Chapter 6
Recognition

Read Esther chapter 6

Discuss/think about

Can you remember a time when you did a 'good deed' and it was rewarded? Can you also remember doing something that nobody seemed to notice? Maybe it was rewarded later or maybe you are still waiting for recognition and reward. How do you feel about this?

1. We sometimes speak about God's sovereignty or the providence of God. List/discuss as many things in this chapter as you can, which are evidence of God working 'behind the scenes'.

2. Why do you think it took so long for the king to find out and reward Mordecai for his actions?

3. Has God ever directed you through a seemingly minor incident in your life? If so how?

4. In what other ways have you felt God directing your life?

5. Why did Haman think the reward was for him?

6. Read Galatians 6:7. How do you think this scripture might apply to what is happening in this chapter?

7. Do we always see a man/woman reaping what he/she sows? How does this make you feel?

8. Why do you think Haman's wife and his advisors said what they did to him in verse 13?

9. Look at Proverbs 11:2. Can you see evidence of this in this chapter and if so, how? Can you think of other Proverbs or

scriptures which might apply here in this chapter or in what you have studied in this book of Esther so far?

10. What have you learned from this chapter about recognition and the ways in which God can work?

Don't forget to pray

Do you ever overlook good deeds which are done, from which you benefit? Think back over your life and the things that different people have done for you in the past – and the present. Write them down, or go over them with God and thank Him for them. Remember to thank the appropriate people too!

Notes for Esther - Chapter 6
Recognition

There are many examples in this chapter of the providence of God at work. The king could not sleep; he asked for the book of the chronicles to be read to him (a most peculiar choice but perhaps he thought it would send him to sleep!); the king realising that Mordecai should have been honoured a long time ago; Haman (rather than anyone else) being in the outer court and arriving at just that moment to ask the king about hanging Mordecai and so on. We sometimes speak about 'luck' or 'coincidence' but perhaps we should stop and consider whether it is God at work in our lives.

We are not told why Mordecai's good deed had been written down but not rewarded and then forgotten. However, we do know that if he had been rewarded five years earlier (when the deed occurred) then the event recorded in this chapter would not have occurred. Perhaps we often wonder why God does not do as we think He should at a particular moment in time. We see only the immediate picture, and especially how it affects us, but we must learn to trust Him because He is working out many things and He is in charge. God had the day already appointed when Mordecai would be honoured. God's timing is always right - Romans 5:6.

In his pride and arrogance Haman thought the honour was for him and we should always be careful not to think more of ourselves than we should (Philippians 2.3)! We are told in Galatians 6 that we reap what we sow (irrespective of whether we are Christians or not) and we can see the truth of this portrayed with Mordecai and Haman. We might think that God does not notice, but this scripture will eventually be true in every life, even if *we* do not actually see it. Galatians 6:7 should encourage us but also make us careful in the way we live our own lives. There is an old saying 'Though the mills of God grind slowly, yet they grind exceeding small; though with patience He stands waiting, yet with exactness grinds He all'. The 'mills' refer to grinding mills which are designed to break down solid material into small parts.

Maybe Haman's wife and advisors knew of Jewish history, maybe they had heard about God's covenant with Abraham, but in any case it was significant for them that Mordecai was a Jew. They were, in effect, warning Haman of what could now happen. God is not willing that any should perish (2 Peter 3:9) and He does warn people and give them opportunities for repentance. Perhaps if Haman had humbled himself and repented of his horrible plans, even at this late stage, there could have been a different outcome and not only he, but also his ten sons (chapter 9) could have been saved.

There are many examples of scriptures which can be seen working out in the book of Esther. Some of these are as follows:- Numbers 32:23 (be sure your sin will find you out); Psalm 7:15; Proverbs 21:1; 2 Chronicles 7:14; Proverbs 16:1; Proverbs 19:21; Genesis 12:2-3 and many more.

Study 9 – Esther Chapter 7
Justice

Read Esther chapter 7

Discuss/think about

How do you react in situations which are clearly unjust? Do you rush in and try and sort it out; stay silent; or bring it to God in prayer and ask Him to intervene and show you if there is anything you should do? Think about any examples of these reactions you have seen or experienced personally. What were the outcomes?

1. As Esther spoke to the king in this chapter and exposed Haman she was also implicating the king in being involved in a terrible crime. How do you think she felt as she finally came to the time when she had to speak?

2. Have you ever had to prepare to speak at a very important time or to a very important person? How did you feel and how did you deal with your feelings?

3. How did God help Esther with her request to the king?

4. If Esther had not acted with such wisdom in this chapter and in previous chapters, could there have been a different outcome?

5. What do you think was going through the king's mind while Esther was putting her request to him?

6. Look at Psalm 49:16-20. Does this apply to anyone in this chapter?

7. How did Haman react when he heard what Esther said? Do you think he was 'repentant'?

8. Can you think of any similarities in the Bible, or in history, of justice eventually catching up with an evil man?

9. Haman was allowed to go on for a long time before God eventually acted through Esther to thwart his plans. Why do you think God often allows a long period of time before He eventually acts?

10. Is there a situation in your life, or in the life of someone else you know, where you feel you are having to wait for justice to prevail? If you are studying in a group maybe you could share this and spend some time in prayer together about it. If you are studying alone ask God for patience while He works everything out.

Don't forget to pray

Ask the Holy Spirit to give you patience while you wait for situations you do not understand to be resolved. Take time to come before your Heavenly Father and ask Him to give you His wisdom so that you know when, or if, you should act.

Notes for Esther - Chapter 7
Justice

Perhaps Esther had rehearsed in her own mind exactly what she was going to say and she would certainly have been praying and asking God about it. In chapter 4:16 she had already said, 'I and my maids will fast as you do'. God must surely have given her special wisdom and understanding in how best to approach the king. She waited for the king to ask her again about her petition and even then she did not simply blurt out that Haman wanted to kill all the Jews.

Esther focused on the fact that she was the king's wife and 'if I have found favour with you' and asked him to spare her life. This was a very sincere request since her life was at stake in two respects. If Haman had been allowed to kill all the Jews then it would only have been a matter of time before it was discovered she was a Jew. In addition to this, the king could easily have been angered by her 'interference' and commanded she be put to death. He had no mercy with Vashti when she angered him, why should it be any different with Esther? The difference however was that Esther had God on her side (Romans 8:31). The outcome could have been so different if Esther had tried to deal with it by herself without prayer and fasting.

Esther's words must have come as a real shock to the king. Who would want to kill his beautiful wife? In addition to this he had just honoured Mordecai, *a Jew*, who had saved the king's life and now he realised he had ordered that all Jews should be killed!

It must also have come as a shock to Haman to realise that Esther was a Jewess! Suddenly all Haman's wealth and privileged status meant absolutely nothing and he could do nothing except plead for his life. Haman was terrified but there is still no indication that he had any acceptance of the terrible thing he had tried to do. He seemed to be simply afraid for his life rather than sorry for what he had done. If Haman had heeded the warnings which had already come to him from his wife and advisors he may have been saved. God does not want anyone to perish but He does want everyone to come to repentance – 2 Peter 3:9.

We should not take God's long-suffering for granted as if He does not notice or does not care. 'The Lord is not slow in keeping His promise, as some understand slowness. He is patient, with you, not wanting anyone to perish, but everyone to come to repentance' 2 Peter 3.9. Peter goes on to say 'the day of the Lord WILL come.......', and justice will be done in God's time.

There are important personal lessons in this chapter as well as a lesson about the Jews and the nation of Israel. God has said in Genesis 12:3 'I will bless those who bless you and whoever curses you I will curse'. Whether it be Pharaoh in Egypt, or Nebuchadnezzar, or Haman or Hitler or anyone else – they will not succeed against God's word. God may not approve of everything that Israel does, but He is faithful and will always keep His word.

God is never in a hurry and is not bound by time. He will, however, always fulfil His plans and purposes. We have already seen it was many years before Mordecai was rewarded. We should also note that it was not until the third year of his reign that the king banished Vashti. Another four years then elapsed before Esther became queen. It was then not until the twelfth year of the king's reign that Haman hatched his plot.

We may not understand why God allows certain situations to continue but we can trust in His love. In all that happens in our lives therefore we can rely on the promises of God. 'God is faithful' – (Deuteronomy 7:9; 1 Corinthians 1:9) and 'if God is for us who can be against us' (Romans 8:28-39).

Study 10 – Esther Chapters 8-10
Faithfulness

Read Esther chapters 8, 9 and 10

Discuss/think about

Esther loved her people and was willing to make great sacrifices for them. She could not rest while their lives were still in danger. Can you see any similarities with this and the Christian message today?

1. Esther interceded on behalf of her people and there was a wonderful result. Can you think of others in the Bible who have acted in a similar way?

2. Look at the following scriptures: Exodus 32:31-32; Romans 9:3; Nehemiah 1:3-4; Daniel 9.:2-3. Can you see any similarities with the book of Esther?

3. How important is prayer today when taking the message of God's love to those who do not know Him? How important is fasting today?

4. What did the king's new orders allow the Jewish people to do?

5. Why had the Gentiles become afraid of the Jews?

6. Look at Acts 9:10; 2 Corinthians 5:11 and Revelation 15:4. Can you see any similarities with the 'fear' mentioned in chapter 9?

7. Do you think the world today has any 'fear of the Lord'?

8. How has the situation changed for the Jews from the beginning of the book of Esther to the end?

9. Why do you think God's name is not mentioned once in the book of Esther?

10. How are Ruth and Esther examples for all Christians to follow?

Don't forget to pray

Ask God to give you, by His Holy Spirit, a real love for other people so that you are willing to intercede for them so that they will come to know God through our Lord Jesus Christ. Ask yourself how much time you are willing to give up to pray (and fast?) for them. Pray that God will ensure that you do not just forget what you have learned from Ruth and Esther but that He will use it to help you to be more committed to Him and to live for His glory and praise.

Notes for Esther - Chapters 8-10
Faithfulness

There are several examples of people in the Bible who have interceded before God for their people with marvellous results – some examples of relevant scriptures are shown in question 2 of the study.

Chapter 8 begins with Esther weeping but ends with joy and gladness among the Jews. What a wonderful result we see from Esther's faithfulness and love for her people. The book of Ruth begins with three funerals and ends with a wedding and a new baby. We can see many similarities when looking at Ruth and Esther. Both women were prepared to commit themselves totally to God and to His will for their lives and both were honoured by God and saw a tremendous result for His glory. However, as they stepped out in faith they could not be sure what would happen and both were prepared to risk everything in order to be faithful. What an example they are to us – to men and women alike. Characteristics such as faithfulness, love, wisdom and so on, can be seen in either men or women.

Everything that Esther had could not satisfy her as long as her people were still in danger. Perhaps we should sometimes ask ourselves whether we are simply thankful for our own salvation and not too worried about anyone else. If we were more committed to prayer and fasting before God for the salvation of others perhaps we would see more results for His glory.

The laws of the Medes and Persians were unalterable so the king could not revoke the previous law against the Jews. However, the king could issue a new decree that favoured the Jews and this would let everyone know what he thought about them. The Jews were given the authority and permission to defend themselves although they were not allowed to be the aggressors.

Perhaps if more of us were prepared to commit ourselves faithfully to God and to be more like Mordecai and Esther then we too would see a great revival today. Are we prepared to surrender ourselves to

God and to His will so that He can work through us for the salvation of others and for His glory?

The Gentiles may have feared the Jews (chapter 9:2) for several reasons. They could see from their present day, and from history, how the God of the Jews took care of them. Perhaps too the Jews found a new courage from what had happened and this in itself would give the Gentiles cause to fear. We should also remember that God is able to put fear into the hearts of men and He may well have acted directly in putting this fear into the hearts of the Gentiles in order to stop them fighting the Jews. There are other references in the Old Testament to the enemies of the Jews having a fear of them – see Genesis 35:5; Deuteronomy 2:25 and Joshua 2:8-11 and 5:1 for examples.

It is good to have a right 'fear' of the Lord and the scriptures noted in question 2 refer to this. Perhaps if we had a greater fear of the Lord today it would affect our lives more so that unbelievers would fear God and want to seek after Him. Wouldn't it be a good thing if the world had a right 'fear' of the Church because they could see the way in which it was so committed to doing God's will. Certainly if the leaders of countries all over the world feared God then many of them would behave in a different way.

There was a remarkable change in, and for, the Jews from the beginning to the end of Esther. The Jews had been mourning and fasting but now they were feasting and rejoicing. At the beginning of the book of Esther they seemed to be keeping a low profile and Mordecai and Esther had not even made it known that they were Jews. We are told at the end of chapter 8 that there were now many other people in the land who wanted to become Jews. This was, of course, because God was protecting the Jews and acting on their behalf in order to preserve them and keep His covenant with them.

We should also remember that God acted through Mordecai and Esther. It has been well said that 'all that is required for evil to triumph is for good men/women to do nothing'. What a wonderful transformation has taken place because of all that Mordecai and Esther had been prepared to do.

The word 'purim' comes from the word 'pur' (in Babylonian) which means 'lot'. The origin of this is thought to be from Haman's casting of lots to decide when the Jews would be destroyed (3:7 and 9:24). The Jews were determined that future generations would not forget the way in which God had delivered them.

Meaningful traditions are a good thing if they cause us to remember the ways in which God has acted in the past, and thus strengthen our faith, trust and understanding of His ways. Christians have many traditions e.g. Easter and Christmas. There are also other traditions which we celebrate in different nations - e.g. Remembrance Day in the UK, so that we do not forget those in the past who have lost their lives for our benefit today.

Although God's name is not mentioned in this book there is no doubt that He is present and active, working everything out according to His will (Ephesians 1:11). Some scholars have suggested that God is not named because the Jewish nation was displeasing to Him at that time and was under a time of His discipline. We do not know for sure, but we can see that both the books of Ruth and Esther are wonderful examples of Romans 8:28. What a great encouragement this should be to us today. Psalm 22:28 says 'for dominion belongs to the Lord and He rules over the nations'. As we look around us today it is easy to despair at the state of things in the world but we should remember that ultimately God is in control and He can achieve great things through one person who is prepared to commit him/herself to Him.

Chapter 10 is a wonderful tribute to the faithfulness of Mordecai. The man who was overlooked earlier in the story is now second in rank to King Xerxes. We may be overlooked by those around us but God knows everything we do for Him. That should be all we need!

We have seen God working through Ruth, Esther and Mordecai because they were prepared to commit themselves to Him and do His will irrespective of the consequences. We have seen God overruling the mind and actions of King Xerxes in order to accomplish His plans and purposes. God can do all this through different people but at the same time He never takes away our freewill. The question for each of us today is am I prepared to give up MY will, in order to commit myself completely to God to do HIS will?

Note from the Author

You have come to the end of this study for Ruth and Esther. You may now wish to study another book in the BSBP series. You will find more information about all the books available in this series on Amazon or on the following website: www.howdoiknowbooks.com

However, having studied Ruth and Esther using the BSBP method you may now wish to go deeper into the Word. There are many Bible studies available and many commentaries from which to choose which would be very beneficial for spiritual growth.

In this study I have tried to summarize the main points of Ruth and Esther as I see them. There is so much more to learn and my prayer is that this study may have given you the desire to go further.

Margaret Weston
https://www.amazon.com/author/margaretweston

Margaret Weston is the author of the BSBP series and the 'How do I know?' series. Information about all the books available and contact details are available on the following website:

www.howdoiknowbooks.com

3803467R00032

Printed in Great Britain
by Amazon.co.uk, Ltd.,
Marston Gate.